Rápido, más rápido, muy rápido

Animales que se mueven a grandes velocidades

por/by
Michael Dahl
ilustrado por/illustrated by
Brian Jensen

Fast, Faster, Fastest

Animals That Move at Great Speeds

PICTURE WINDOW BOOKS
a capstone imprint

Editor: Christianne Jones
Translation Services: Strictly Spanish
Story Consultant: Terry Flaherty
Designer: Nathan Gassman
Bilingual Book Designer: Eric Manske
Production Artist: Danielle Ceminsky
Page Production: Picture Window Books
The illustrations in this book were created with pastels.

Picture Window Books
A Capstone Imprint
1710 Roe Crest Drive
North Mankato, MN 56003
www.capstonepub.com

Library of Congress Cataloging-in-Publication Data
Dahl, Michael.
 [Fast, faster, fastest. Spanish & English]
 Rápido, más rápido, muy rápido : animales que se mueven a grandes
velocidades / por Michael Dahl ; ilustrado por Brian Jensen = Fast,
faster, fastest : animals that move at great speeds / by Michael Dahl ;
illustrated by Brian Jensen.
     p. cm.—(Picture window bilingüe. Los extremos y los animales =
Bilingual picture window. Animal extremes)
 Includes index.
 Summary: "Describes some animals that move at extreme speeds
when they jump, run, or fly—in both English and Spanish"—Provided by
publisher.
 ISBN 978-1-4048-7317-9 (library binding)
 1. Animal locomotion—Juvenile literature. I. Jensen, Brian, ill. II. Title.
III. Title: Fast, faster, fastest.
QP301.D24318 2012
591.5'7—dc23   2011028280

Thanks to our advisers for their expertise, research, and advice:

Dr. James F. Hare, Associate Professor of Zoology
University of Manitoba
Winnipeg, Manitoba

Susan Kesselring, M.A., Literacy Educator
Rosemount-Apple Valley-Eagan (Minnesota) School District

Printed in the United States of America in North Mankato, Minnesota.
102011   006405CGS12

Animals live everywhere. They fly over the highest mountains and swim in the deepest oceans. They run over the hottest deserts and dive into the coldest waters.

Don't blink, or you might miss these animals that can move at extreme speeds. Watch the needle move across the speedometer as you turn each page.

Los animales viven en todas partes. Ellos vuelan sobre las montañas más altas y nadan en los océanos más profundos. Ellos corren por los desiertos más calientes y se sumergen en las aguas más frías.

No pestañees o te perderás estos animales que se mueven a velocidades extremas. Mira cómo se mueve la aguja en el velocímetro cada vez que das vuelta la página.

Hop! Hop! Hop!

¡Salta! ¡Salta! ¡Salta!

The kangaroo bounces 35 mph across the dusty deserts of Australia.

El canguro rebota a 35 mph a través de los polvorientos desiertos de Australia.

Can any animal move faster?

¿Puede algún otro animal moverse más rápido?

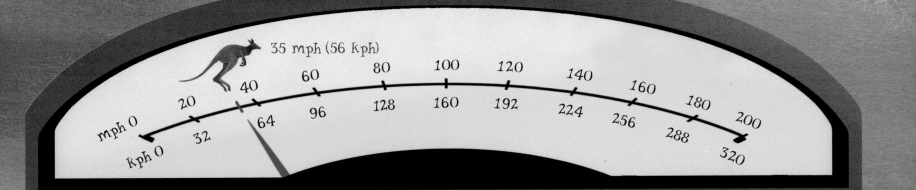

35 mph (56 kph)

mph 0   20   40   60   80   100   120   140   160   180   200

Kph 0   32   64   96   128   160   192   224   256   288   320

divertidos

white-throated needle-tailed swift/ vencejo mongol

The white-throated needle-tailed swift spends most of its life in the air. It never lands on the ground on purpose.

El vencejo mongol se pasa la mayoría de su vida en el aire. Nunca aterriza en el suelo a propósito.

bald eagle/ águila calva

Bald eagles aren't bald. Their heads are covered with short white feathers.

Las águilas calvas no son calvas. Sus cabezas están cubiertas de plumas blancas cortas.

peregrine falcon/ halcón peregrino

Peregrine falcons nest on every continent except Antarctica. They leave their nests in the winter, but return to the same nest each summer.

El halcón peregrino anida en cada continente excepto en Antártida. Ellos dejan sus nidos en el invierno, pero vuelven al mismo nido cada verano.

Glossary
plains—flat land with few trees
savanna—flat, grassy plain with few trees
sprint—to run fast for a short distance
swoop—to dive down suddenly
whisk—to move quickly

Glosario
apresurar—moverse más rápidamente
bajar en picada—volar hacia abajo rápidamente
esprintar —correr rápidamente por una
    distancia corta
las planicies—tierra llana con pocos árboles
la sabana—planicie plana y con pasto con
    pocos árboles

Internet Sites

FactHound offers a safe, fun way to find Internet sites related to this book. All of the sites on FactHound have been researched by our staff.

Here's all you do:

Visit *www.facthound.com*

Type in this code: 9781404873179

 **Super-cool stuff!** Check out projects, games and lots more at **www.capstonekids.com**

Sitios de Internet

FactHound brinda una forma segura y divertida de encontrar sitios de Internet relacionados con este libro. Todos los sitios en FactHound han sido investigados por nuestro personal.

Esto es todo lo que tienes que hacer:

Visita *www.facthound.com*

Ingresa este código: 9781404873179

 **¡Algo súper divertido!** Hay proyectos, juegos y mucho más en **www.capstonekids.com**